FIND OUT ABOUT

Wood

© 1994 Watts Books

Watts Books
96 Leonard Street
London EC2A 4RH

Franklin Watts Australia
14 Mars Road
Lane Cove
NSW 2066

UK ISBN: 0 7496 1632 6

10 9 8 7 6 5 4 3 2 1

Dewey Decimal Classification 333.75

A CIP catalogue record for this book
is available from the British Library

Editor: Annabel Martin
Design: Thumb Design

Photographs: © English Heritage 19;
Eye Ubiquitous © Hugh Rooney 25 (inset);
Chris Fairclough Colour Library 6, 7, 8, 10,
11, 12, 13, 14, 15, 16, 17, 20, 21, 23, 25, 27,
29 (both); Robert Harding Picture Library 22,
© Christopher Nicholson 24, © Sarah King 28;
The Hutchison Library 30, © Edward Parker 4,
© Val Whelan 9, © John Wright 31; National
Trust Photographic Library 18, © J.Whitaker 26;
ZEFA 5.

Printed in Hong Kong

FIND OUT ABOUT

Henry Pluckrose

Watts Books

London • New York • Sydney

Wood comes from trees.
Trees grow all over the world.
They grow in hot, damp
lands of Africa, Asia
and South America.

They also grow in lands where winters are very cold.

In some countries
forests are specially planted.
Saplings, which are little trees,
are planted in long rows.

When they are fully grown, the trees are cut down. The branches are trimmed from the trees.

At the saw mill,
the trunks are cut into planks …

and dried.
Dried wood is called timber.

Many different tools are used for cutting and shaping wood. Saws cut it, planes smooth it, chisels cut into it and decorate it, lathes turn and shape it, drills make holes in it.

Most of the tools
we use to shape timber
are made of metal.
Can you think why?

Pieces of wood
can be fixed together
with nails, screws
or glue.

Another way of fixing pieces of wood together is to make a joint. The shapes cut into each piece of wood fit neatly into each other.

Woodwork must be protected
from water, rain and sun.
Wooden things are painted
to prevent them from rotting.

Furniture is waxed and polished to protect the wooden surface from spills of food and drink.

Wood is a very useful material. It can be used in many ways – to build real houses …

and to make toy ones!

Most wood is tough
and long lasting.
This table is over 500 years old ...

and this chair was made
long before your grandmother
was born.

Many other things in our homes
are made from wood —
the handles of brushes, brooms,
kitchen knives, cooking spoons,
salad and fruit bowls,
cutting boards.

Why do we use a wooden mat
to protect a polished table
from a hot dish?
The metal spoon lets heat
pass through it easily.
Metal is a good conductor of heat.
The wooden handle
stays cool because
wood is a poor conductor of heat.

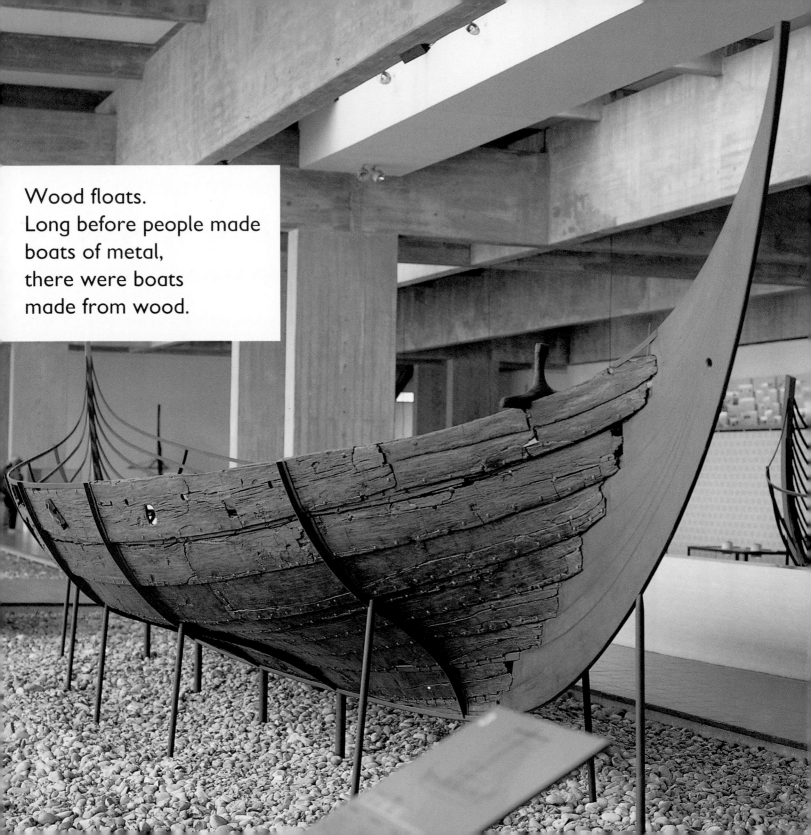

Wood floats.
Long before people made
boats of metal,
there were boats
made from wood.

Wood is a tough material.
It is used to build quays
where ships tie up
to unload their cargo.

Some kinds of wheels are still made from wood. The rim of the wheel is given a metal shoe to prevent the wood from wearing away.

Many musical instruments can be made from wood.

Wood is soft enough
to carve.
Some old houses
are decorated with
wood carvings.
This carving was made
over 300 years ago.

Wood is also used to make
decorations for people.
Would you like to wear
these beads?

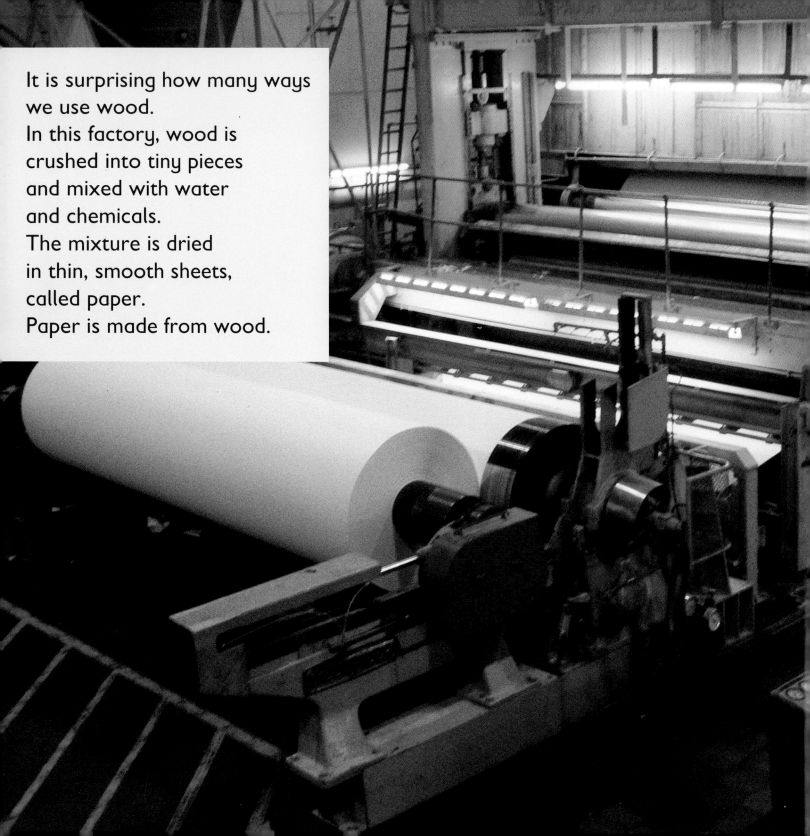

It is surprising how many ways
we use wood.
In this factory, wood is
crushed into tiny pieces
and mixed with water
and chemicals.
The mixture is dried
in thin, smooth sheets,
called paper.
Paper is made from wood.

We even need
wood to make pencils!

Trees which give us wood
take many years to grow.
In some parts of the world,
large areas of forests
are being cut down.
The wood is sold
and the land left empty.

When this happens,
the soil is often washed away
and nothing can grow.
We must learn to care
for the world of nature.
Can you imagine
the countryside with no trees?

About this book

This book is designed for use in the home, kindergarten and infant school.

Parents can share the book with young children. Its aim is to bring into focus some of the elements of life and living which are all too often taken for granted. To develop fully, all young children need to have their understanding of the world deepened and the language they use to express their ideas extended. This book, and others in the series, takes the everyday things of the child's world and explores them, harnessing curiosity and wonder in a purposeful way.

For those working with young children each book is designed to be used both as a picture book, which explores ideas and concepts, and as a starting point to talk and exploration. The pictures have been selected because they are of interest in themselves and also because they include elements which will promote enquiry. Talk can lead to displays of items and pictures collected by children and teacher. Pictures and collages can be made by the children themselves.

Everything in our environment is of interest to the growing child. The purpose of these books is to extend and develop that interest.

Henry Pluckrose

GREAT
OLYMPIC
MOMENTS

Michael Hurley

www.raintreepublishers.co.uk

Visit our website to find out more information about Raintree books.

To order:

☎ Phone 0845 6044371

🖷 Fax +44 (0) 1865 312263

🖳 Email myorders@raintreepublishers.co.uk

Customers from outside the UK please telephone +44 1865 312262

Raintree is an imprint of Capstone Global Library Limited, a company incorporated in England and Wales having its registered office at 7 Pilgrim Street, London, EC4V 6LB – Registered company number: 6695582

Text © Capstone Global Library Limited 2012
First published in hardback in 2012
The moral rights of the proprietor have been asserted.

Edited by Kate de Villiers and Laura Knowles
Designed by Richard Parker
Picture research by Liz Alexander
Production by Camilla Crask
Originated by Capstone Global Library Ltd
Printed and bound in China by CTPS

ISBN 978 1 406 22398 9 (hardback)
15 14 13 12 11
10 9 8 7 6 5 4 3 2 1

British Library Cataloguing in Publication Data
Hurley, Michael.
Great Olympic moments. -- (The Olympics)
796.4'8-dc22
A full catalogue record for this book is available from the British Library.

Acknowledgements
We would like to thank the following for permission to reproduce photographs: Alamy pp. **16** (© Associated Sports Photography), **4 left** (© Mary Evans Picture Library); Corbis pp. **10** (© Bettmann), **4 right** (© How Hwee Young/epa); Getty Images pp. **7** (Central Press/Hulton Archive), **9** (Shaun Botterill /Allsport), **11** (Popperfoto), **12** (Steve Powell), **13** (Mark Carwell/AFP), **17** (Jerry Cooke/Sports Illustrated), **18** (Pascal Pavani/AFP), **21** (Romeo Gacad/AFP), **23** (Keystone /Hulton Archive), **25** (Tony Duffy); Press Association Images p. **15** (AP Photo/Rusty Kennedy), Reuters p. **19** (Bruno Domingos).

Cover photograph of Derartu Tulu and Elana Meyer reproduced with permission of Getty Images/John Iacono/Sports Illustrated.

Every effort has been made to contact copyright holders of material reproduced in this book. Any omissions will be rectified in subsequent printings if notice is given to the publishers.

Disclaimer
All the internet addresses (URLs) given in this book were valid at the time of going to press. However, due to the dynamic nature of the internet, some addresses may have changed, or sites may have changed or ceased to exist since publication. While the author and publisher regret any inconvenience this may cause readers, no responsibility for any such changes can be accepted by either the author or the publisher.

Contents

Some words are shown in bold, **like this**. You can find them in the glossary on page 30.

World of Olympics

The Olympic Games are based on the games that were held every **Olympiad** (four years) in **Ancient Greece**. The Olympics have been held every four years since 1896, except during the two World Wars (1914–1918 and 1939–1945).

The Olympics feature athletes from around the world competing against each other in various different sports. Track and field events include sprinting, high jump, and javelin. There are also indoor events such as swimming, cycling, and gymnastics. Other popular Olympic sports include football, tennis, and hockey. There are 38 different sports in total.

Olympic athletes' clothing has changed a lot. Take a look at these **marathon** runners from 1896 (above) compared with athletes in 2008 (right).

There are both Summer and Winter Olympic Games. The Winter Olympics are also held every four years, two years after the Summer Games. The sports in the Winter Olympics are very different. They include downhill and cross-country skiing, ice-skating, and bob-sled.

Athletes with disabilities take part in the **Paralympic Games**. These take place every four years in the same country that hosts the Olympics. Athletes compete in a variety of sports.

Over the years there have been many great moments at the Olympics. However, there have also been some shocking and controversial moments.

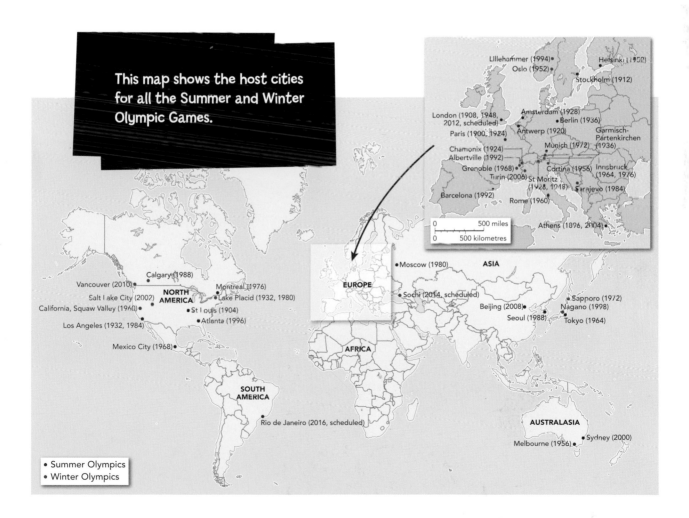

This map shows the host cities for all the Summer and Winter Olympic Games.

Lillehammer (1994)
Oslo (1952)
Helsinki (1952)
Stockholm (1912)
London (1908, 1948, 2012, scheduled)
Amsterdam (1928)
Berlin (1936)
Paris (1900, 1924)
Antwerp (1920)
Garmisch-Partenkirchen (1936)
Chamonix (1924)
Munich (1972)
Albertville (1992)
Grenoble (1968)
Cortina (1956)
Innsbruck (1964, 1976)
Turin (2006)
St Moritz (1928, 1948)
Sarajevo (1984)
Barcelona (1992)
Rome (1960)
Athens (1896, 2004)

0   500 miles
0   500 kilometres

Calgary (1988)
Vancouver (2010)
Montreal (1976)
EUROPE
Moscow (1980)
ASIA
Salt Lake City (2002)
NORTH AMERICA
Lake Placid (1932, 1980)
Sochi (2014, scheduled)
Sapporo (1972)
California, Squaw Valley (1960)
St Louis (1904)
Beijing (2008)
Nagano (1998)
Los Angeles (1932, 1984)
Atlanta (1996)
Seoul (1988)
Tokyo (1964)
Mexico City (1968)
AFRICA

SOUTH AMERICA

Rio de Janeiro (2016, scheduled)
AUSTRALASIA
Sydney (2000)
Melbourne (1956)

• Summer Olympics
• Winter Olympics

Amazing moments

Every Olympic Games includes some amazing moments. The achievements of individuals can inspire and excite audiences around the world. From the bizarre to the heroic, these moments are remembered as part of Olympic history.

Eric the eel

In 2000 Eric Moussambani competed in the Sydney Olympics. The swimmer from Equitorial Guinea in Africa was not used to swimming more than 50 metres. At the Olympics he had to swim 100 metres. He was also the only person in the pool after other competitors were **disqualified** for false starts. The crowd cheered on Moussambani as he slowly finished his race and became an Olympic star. Later he said, "I could hear them cheering and it helped me to get to the end." His unusual swimming style earned him the nickname "Eric the eel".

Recovering from tragedy

Dan Jansen's sister died from leukaemia a few hours before he competed at the 1988 Winter Olympics. The US speed skater was favourite to win gold but fell during the race. Days later he fell again in another race. It was too difficult for him to compete after such a tragic loss.

At the 1994 Olympics in Lillehammer, Norway, Jansen won a gold medal in speed skating and dedicated his win to his sister. The crowd applauded as he took his young daughter with him on his victory lap. His daughter was named Jane, after his sister.

Muhammad Ali (second from the right) was only 18 years old when he won a gold medal for boxing at the 1960 Olympics in Rome. Ali went on to become perhaps the greatest boxer in history and one of the most recognizable sportsmen in the world.

Usain Bolt

Winning the 100-metre Olympic title is a fantastic achievement. To win Olympic gold and break the world record is extremely special. Jamaican sprinter Usain ("Lightning") Bolt did both at the 2008 Olympics in Beijing, China. Bolt was so far ahead of the other competitors that he even slowed down as he crossed the finish line!

Cathy Freeman

The sight of Australian Cathy Freeman running in her green and gold hooded suit is one of the most memorable Olympic moments. Freeman was under intense pressure to win the 400-metre gold at the Sydney Olympics in 2000. It was a very close race but in the final 50 metres Freeman took the lead and she won by several metres. The crowd in the Olympic stadium went wild!

Five gold medals

At the Sydney Olympics in 2000, Steve Redgrave became the first British athlete to win a gold medal at five **consecutive** Olympics. As part of two-man and four-man rowing teams, Redgrave proved himself to be one of the greatest athletes of all time. Redgrave and his teammates had to push themselves to the limit to win in Sydney. With a few hundred metres left, it looked as though they would be denied gold, but a final push meant that they won by just over half a second!

Steve Redgrave holds up his fifth Olympic gold medal for rowing. His haul of five gold medals makes him one of the greatest Olympians of all time.

Controversial moments

In the history of the Olympics, some athletes have had to perform in difficult and unfair circumstances.

Shock for Hitler

The 1936 Olympics were held in Berlin, Germany. At the time, Adolf Hitler was the German leader. He wanted to use the Olympics to show how skilled and powerful German athletes were compared to those from other countries. Hitler's plan did not work. The outstanding performance of the 1936 Olympics came from Jesse Owens, an African-American athlete. Owens won four gold medals.

Jesse Owens leads the other competitors as he races towards another gold medal at the 1936 Olympics.

Racial differences

Incredibly, when Jesse Owens returned to the United States he did not receive much attention. At that time black people were treated differently from white people. This was known as **segregation**. At the 1968 Olympics in Mexico, two US medal winners used the medal ceremony to highlight the fact that black people were still being treated differently in their country. After they received their medals they each raised one fist wearing a black leather glove. The gloves represented the black people's fight for **equality** in the United States.

US athletes Tommie Smith (middle) and John Carlos make their protest at the medal ceremony for the 200 metres.

Skater attack!

Before the 1994 Winter Olympics, the US ice skater Nancy Kerrigan was assaulted and injured. It was proved that she had been attacked by someone hired by the ex-husband of another US ice skater, Tonya Harding. Harding was worried about losing to her rival. Kerrigan recovered well enough to compete and won a silver medal. Harding finished in eighth place.

Surprise results

Often the team or athletes who are expected to win do take home the Olympic medals. Sometimes, however, the Olympics can produce a surprise result.

Miracle on ice

One of the most surprising results happened when the United States beat the **Soviet Union** at ice hockey in 1980. The Soviet Union was expected to win. Ice hockey was a sport they had **dominated** for many years. The United States was the **underdog**. By the end of the second period, the US team was losing 3–2. But in the third period the US team started to play faster and more aggressively and scored twice to take a 4–3 lead. They held back the Soviet team for the last ten minutes of the match and won. The US players and their fans were overjoyed. The result was so unexpected that it was called "the miracle on ice".

After beating the Soviet Union, the US ice hockey team beat Finland 4-2 in the final match to win the gold medal.

Eddie the eagle

At the Calgary Winter Olympics in 1988, Michael Edwards from the United Kingdom finished last in the ski jump competition. This was no surprise as there were no ski jumps in the UK where he could practise. The surprise was that Edwards could compete at all. He became a hero for many who loved to see his obvious enthusiasm for the sport. They gave him the nickname "Eddie the eagle".

Michael "Eddie the eagle" Edwards in mid-air during one of his ski jumps at the 1988 Winter Olympics in Calgary, Canada.

Multiple medallists

At the Olympics there have been some truly outstanding individual achievements. Some athletes are just happy to take part, which is what the Olympics are really all about. Others are thrilled to win a medal of any sort. Some athletes are determined to win gold again, and again, and again! Here are some famous Olympic champions:

Name: Jesse Owens
Born: 1913, Oakville, Alabama, USA
Medals: Four gold
　　　　 Jesse Owens was the first athlete to win four gold medals at a single Olympics.

Name: Fanny Blankers-Koen
Born: 1918, Baarn, Netherlands
Medals: Four gold
　　　　 Dutch woman Fanny Blankers-Koen was the first woman to win four gold medals at a single Olympics when she competed in the 1948 London Olympic Games.

Name: Frederick Carlton Lewis (Carl Lewis)
Born: 1961, Birmingham, Alabama, USA
Medals: Nine gold, one silver
　　　　 Carl Lewis won four gold medals at the 1984 Olympics in Los Angeles.

Name: Mark Spitz
Born: 1950, Modesto, California, USA
Medals: Nine gold, one silver, one bronze
　　　　 In the 1972 Munich Olympics, swimmer Mark Spitz became the first person to win seven golds at a single Olympics.

Name: Mustapha Badid
Born: France
Medals: Five gold
At the 1988
Paralympic Games
in Seoul, wheelchair
racer Mustapha Badid
won four gold medals
for wheelchair racing.

Name: Ian Thorpe
Born: 1982, Sydney, New South Wales, Australia
Medals: Five gold, three silver, one bronze
Seventeen-year-old Australian swimmer Ian Thorpe gained
the nickname "Thorpedo" after winning three gold and
two silver medals at the 2000 Olympic Games in Sydney.

Name: Ole Einar Bjørndalen
Born: 1974, Drammen, Norway
Medals: Six gold, four silver, one bronze
Ole Einar Bjorndalen won four gold medals in the biathlon
at the 2002 Winter Olympics in Salt Lake City.

Name: Kelly Holmes
Born: 1970, Pembury, Kent, United Kingdom
Medals: Two gold, one bronze
When she won two gold medals in Athens in 2004, Kelly
Holmes became the first British woman since 1956 to win
multiple gold medals at a single Olympics.

Repeat success

Winning a gold medal at one Olympics is special, but to win gold at **consecutive** Olympics is amazing. The following athletes have managed to achieve this incredible feat:

- Aladar Gerevich, from Hungary, won gold medals in fencing at six consecutive Olympics (1932, 1936, 1948, 1952, 1956, and 1960).

- Lasse Viren, a Finnish long distance runner, won the 5,000-metres and the 10,000-metres gold medal at the 1972 and 1976 Olympics.

- Nadia Comaneci from Romania won multiple gold medals in gymnastics at the 1976 and 1980 Olympics.

US sprinter Michael Johnson won gold in the 400 metres at the 1996 and 2000 Olympics.

Czech gymnast Vera Caslavska took part in three Olympics. After winning a silver medal in 1960, she won three gold medals in 1964 – and four more in 1968!

- Tanni Grey-Thompson won gold medals at four consecutive **Paralympic Games** (1992, 1996, 2000, and 2004).

- Steve Redgrave is the only British male athlete to win a gold medal at five consecutive Olympics. The British rower first won gold at the 1984 games in Los Angeles. He won his fifth and final gold medal at the 2000 Olympics in Sydney.

- US swimmer Michael Phelps is a **phenomenon**! Phelps has won more gold medals than anyone else in Olympic history. He followed up his success in Athens in 2000, where he won six gold medals, by winning eight gold medals in Beijing in 2008.

- US snowboarder Shaun White won gold in the **halfpipe** at the Winter Olympics in 2006 and 2010.

Fair play at the Olympics

The motto of the Olympic games is "*Cituis, Altius, Fortius*". That translates from Latin as "Faster, Higher, Stronger". The motto was created by Pierre de Coubertin, the founder of the modern Olympics. The motto reminds all Olympic competitors that taking part and doing your best are just as important as winning. Athletes are expected to compete fairly and show respect to their rivals.

Lap of honour

At the 1992 Barcelona Olympics the winner of the 10,000 metres was Derartu Tulu from Ethiopia. Derartu was the first black African woman to win an Olympic gold medal. When she finished she waited at the line for Elana Meyer, who came second. Meyer is a white South African. The two women then set off together on a lap of honour. The image of one black and one white African running together to the crowd's applause was a special moment in history.

Derartu Tulu (left) and Elana Meyer hold hands as they take a lap of honour after their 10,000 metres race at the Olympics in Barcelona.

Rewarding fair play

The Olympic Fair Play committee was set up in 1964. The committee gives awards to competitors who show an outstanding example of sportsmanship.

Special award

In 1964, the first ever letter of congratulations for an Act of Fair Play was awarded to the Swedish rowers Lars Gunnar Kall and Stig Lienart Kall by the International Fair Play Committee. The rowers were in an Olympic race for the gold medal but stopped to help other competitors whose boat had capsized.

Brazilian runner Vanderlei de Lima was awarded a Fair Play Trophy after a spectator pushed him during the 2004 Olympic marathon, ruining his chance of winning the race.

Shocking Olympic moments

The Olympic Games have seen moments of great sporting achievement and created heroes around the world. Alongside this success, however, there have been some shocking events.

Drugs at the Olympics

Although the Olympics have produced some amazing athletic performances, some athletes have chosen to use drugs as a way to win. One of the most shocking moments in Olympic history happened in 1988. The winner of the 100 metres, Ben Johnson from Canada, was stripped of his gold medal. He had tested positive for a banned substance a few days after the event.

21st century cheat

Today the problem of athletes using drugs to gain an advantage over their opponents continues. The US sprinter Marion Jones won three gold and two bronze medals at the 2000 Olympics in Sydney. She later had to return the medals because she admitted to using **performance-enhancing drugs**.

Drunk athlete

The first athlete to be **disqualified** for drug use was Swedish pentathlete Hans-Gunner Liljenwall in 1968. He was disqualified for excessive alcohol intake.

Ben Johnson celebrates winning the 100 metres at the Seoul Olympics in 1988. However, he was not smiling a few days later after being stripped of the title.

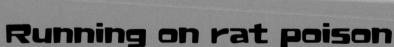

Running on rat poison

Some athletes will do anything to win. The US athlete Thomas Hicks, winner of the 1904 Olympic **marathon**, admitted to using a mixture of egg whites, brandy, and strychnine to improve his performance. Strychnine is the main ingredient in rat poison!

Terrorism at the Olympics

At all major world sporting events the fear of a **terrorist** attack is never very far away. Lots of money is spent on security and everything is done to ensure that the Olympic Games run smoothly. Sometimes, however, tragedy strikes.

Munich, 1972

During the 1972 Olympics, a group of eight Palestinian terrorists broke into the **Olympic Village** where the athletes were staying. Their intention was to kidnap the Israeli athletes. The terrorists were armed and determined. **Negotiations** were held to try to bring the situation to a peaceful end. Unfortunately, they did not succeed and the German police decided to raid the room where the Israelis were being held.

The raid went disastrously wrong. It ended with all the Israeli athletes being killed, along with five terrorists, and one policeman. As a sign of respect the Games were suspended for 36 hours and a memorial service was held in the main stadium. Sadly, the 1972 Olympics will always be remembered more for this awful incident than for the athletes' achievements.

Atlanta, 1996

In 1996 a bomb exploded during a concert held to celebrate the opening of the Atlanta Olympics. The bomb killed one person and injured more than 100 others. Despite this tragedy, the Olympic organizing committee decided to continue with the Games. This prevented the terrorists from achieving their aim of disrupting or stopping the Olympics.

A memorial service is held in the Olympic stadium in Munich for the Israeli athletes murdered by terrorists during the 1972 Olympics.

Olympic boycotts

There have been several occasions when certain countries have decided to **boycott** (not attend) the Olympic Games.

Africans refuse to compete

In 1976, 22 African countries boycotted the Montreal Games to protest against the fact that New Zealand was taking part. The African nations were angry that New Zealand had toured South Africa to play rugby. At the time, South Africa had a policy of **apartheid**. This meant that black people had fewer rights than white people. Most countries around the world would not allow their sporting teams to visit South Africa in protest against apartheid.

United States boycotts Moscow

The United States boycotted the Moscow Olympics in 1980 because they were unhappy that the **Soviet Union** had invaded Afghanistan. The governments of Great Britain and Australia were also not happy with this situation, but allowed their athletes to attend the games.

Anything you can do . . .

The Soviet Union and other **communist** countries, including Cuba and Bulgaria, boycotted the 1984 Olympics in Los Angeles, USA. This was a direct response to the United States not attending the Moscow Olympics four years earlier.

Sport and politics

Sport and politics should not mix, but sometimes sport is used as a way of making a political point. Occasionally this happens when a government prevents athletes from competing at the Olympics. Hopefully, every country will allow their athletes to compete at the 2012 Olympics in London.

This photograph shows the opening ceremony for the 1980 Olympics in Moscow. The United States did not send a team to compete at the Moscow Olympics.

Olympic timeline

1896 Athens, Greece
1900 Paris, France
1904 Saint-Louis, USA
1908 London, UK
1912 Stockholm, Sweden
1920 Antwerp, Belgium
1924 Paris, France
1924 Chamonix, France (W)
1928 Amsterdam, Netherlands
1928 St Moritz, Switzerland (Winter)
1932 Los Angeles, USA
1932 Lake Placid, USA (W)
1936 Berlin
1936 Garmisch-Partenkirchen, Germany (W)
1948 London, UK
1948 St Moritz, Switzerland (W)
1952 Helsinki, Finland
1952 Oslo, Norway (W)
1956 Melbourne, Australia
1956 Cortina, Italy (W)
1960 Rome, Italy
1960 Squaw Valley, USA (W)
1964 Tokyo
1964 Innsbruck, Austria (W)

1904: Gold, silver, and bronze medals are given out for the first time.

1948: Hungarian athlete Karoly Takacs wins gold in the pistol event. During World War II he had his right arm blown off by a grenade. He taught himself to shoot with his left hand.

1900: Women compete for the first time. The first gold medal is won by the British tennis player Charlotte Cooper.

1924: For the first time, the closing ceremony includes raising the flag of the current host nation, future host nation, and the **International Olympic Committee**.

1936: First Olympics to be shown on television. It is seen on giant screens in cinemas in Germany.

1964: The Olympics are held in Asia for the first time.

1932: Electronic timing and photo finishes are introduced.

1896: US athlete James Connolly becomes the first Olympic champion for his performance in the triple jump.

1960: Boxer Clement "Ike" Quartey from Ghana becomes the first black African to win an Olympic medal.

Find out more

Books

Outstanding Olympics, Clive Gifford (Oxford University Press, 2008)

The Olympics: Crises at the Olympics, Haydn Middleton (Heinemann Library, 2008)

The Sports Book (Dorling Kindersley, 2009)

Training to Succeed: Track Athletics, Rita Storey (Franklin Watts, 2009)

Welcome to the Ancient Olympics: Ancient Greece, Jane Bingham (Raintree, 2007)

Websites

www.london2012.com
The website of the London 2012 Games includes details of venues and preparations for the Games as well as information about Olympic sports.

www.olympic.org
The official website of the International Olympic Committee includes facts and statistics about every Olympic Games and every medal winner.

www.paralympic.org
This is the official website of the Paralympic movement.

To find out about the different countries competing at the Olympics, you can search for the National Olympic Committee of each country.

Index